Archbishop Vincent Nichols

Be open to God's Love

First Homilies of the Most Reverend
Vincent Nichols, Archbishop of Westminster

*All booklets are published thanks to the
generous support of the members of the
Catholic Truth Society*

CATHOLIC TRUTH SOCIETY
PUBLISHERS TO THE HOLY SEE

Contents

Our vocation to love

Vespers, 20th May 2009

This evening I am so glad to greet you all. I welcome His Excellency, the Apostolic Nuncio, and His Eminence Cardinal Mahoney who has made the long journey from Los Angeles. Thank you Your Eminence. May I greet in a special way all who are here representing the religious life of the Diocese, and those who are from its schools. We have heard the roll-call of the saints to whom your communities and schools are dedicated. I trust that the saints will join in this great prayer, too. I welcome all from the parishes of the Diocese. Thank you for coming, thank you for your welcome

The words on which I would like to ponder are these words of St Paul: 'Nothing outweighs the supreme advantage of knowing Christ Jesus my Lord' (*Ph* 3:8-9).

This is such a key phrase in our faith. It resonates deeply in the heart of each of us, for we all try to live by that trusting faith as best we can. We are told by the Church that a diocese is incomplete without the presence of women and men who dedicate themselves through poverty, chastity and obedience in the pursuit of this supreme advantage of knowing Christ Jesus. And this Diocese is blessed with a great richness of Religious who live in the service of the Lord.

Knowledge of Christ Jesus

Tomorrow I will try to explore something of the meaning of these words in the public forum. But this evening, within the family of the Church, we can reflect on them in a more personal way.

These words reveal so much of the heart of St Paul. The knowledge of which he speaks is, of course, the knowledge of the heart – that deep mutual knowledge reflected in the love between husband and wife, or in the best of loving friendships. For us all and especially for religious men and women, it's a knowledge rooted in love and explored in love. When we follow this kind of knowledge, when it permeates our very being, when we strive day by day to deepen this loving awareness, then it becomes the centre of our lives. Then, as we face the tasks of each day, we can say quite simply, 'I do it all for you, Lord'.

Love must become action

These words also relate to all that Paul reveals about his ambition. What he strives for is that this knowledge should grow. He says: 'I want only the perfection that comes through faith in Christ'. 'All I want to know is Christ'. This and this alone is our true ambition.

This evening let us seek to renew this deep and personal desire: that at the centre of each one of us we may ponder anew the wonder of this loving, intimate knowledge of the Lord.

This love and knowledge of Christ flows in action. This action is well described as the work of justice. Justice is born when we see everyone with the eyes of love – every person, every human being, every human life – and act accordingly. Our call for the just treatment of every human being is the call of love, the call of the knowledge of the God present in every person.

Justice is born from love

Recently I was reading a book on ethics – or rather struggling with it. Central to its theme was a story set in an Australian psychiatric hospital, some many years ago now. The description told that the nursing staff were somewhat rough and indifferent in the treatment of the residents. The professional staff treated them with great competence, but from a very dispassionate point of view. Then, the story tells, a nun came to work in the hospital. She simply treated each resident, or patient, with unwavering love. Her relationship with each of them became a revelation. It revealed again the true humanity of each resident. And it revealed the shortcomings of their treatment by others. Love was the measure, the yardstick of her work for justice, because such work always starts with hearts turned to God.

Perhaps we are reminded of this truth in the tradition and teaching of the Church that the first demands of justice spell out our duty towards God. The first justice is to know, love, serve and praise God. From this springs the second branch of justice: the responsibilities we have towards others. Indeed we are often reminded that we cannot fully proclaim or show justice towards others without fulfilling the requirements of justice towards God.

Our vocation matures in love

Then there is another phrase in the reading from St Paul which we have heard. He says: 'I forget the past and I strain ahead for what is still to come.' This suggests, to me at least, that the knowledge of the Lord which we seek, and which is at the heart of our vocation, gets keener, more sensitive, more nuanced, as years go by. Indeed, experience suggests that as this love becomes more deeply rooted, more rounded, then we become more ready to follow the will of the Lord and not our own.

One charge that can hardly be laid against the Church is that of being ageist! In fact, in our life as disciples, age is not a problem! This evening I truly salute so many religious women, priests, and many others, who live fully and generously into old age. You are an example and an inspiration to us all. You keep alive that spirit of selfless service, a truly prophetic voice.

Perhaps St Paul goes a bit far when he speaks of 'racing to the finish'! But we at least keep trying, conscious of the Lord's promise that the best still lies ahead. Let's thank God for this hope, to which we may generously witness in our world today.

Unity starts in Christ

As I look around this evening, I see many religious who have worked for long years in this Diocese. You have given your lives in service to the people here. Others are newly arrived, and from far and wide. You are most welcome. Together we make up that rich and varied community which is the Catholic Church in this city today.

Again we listen to the words of Paul when he speaks of 'the supreme advantage of knowing Christ'. This knowledge is our profound unity, our cohesion as the Body of Christ, within which we acknowledge and rejoice in all the richness of our diversity.

I offer my thanks to all who work for this visible unity in diversity within the Church in this Diocese of Westminster.

Education in virtue

May I now address a word to the teachers and pupils present here this evening. Cherish the privilege of working in and for a Catholic school. Always be proud of the opportunities which are yours in Catholic education. Centred on this knowledge of Christ, you work hard at learning the skills and virtues we need in our society today.

We all know, from the life of every school, that regulations are important. Rules have to be in place, and they have to be observed. But regulation alone is never enough. Rather today we need to live by the virtues of honesty, integrity, prudence and courage – virtues which underpin the proper regulation of our transactions. We are a people who seek to live by these virtues. When we do, our witness becomes attractive to others for they can see in us a spirit of service and self-sacrifice that goes beyond every regulation.

Talk of virtues might sound boring. But when virtue is put into practice the outcome is far from dull or deadened.

Think of what we mean when we speak of a 'virtuoso performance' by a musician or footballer. Music without virtuosity can indeed be dull. Nothing enlivens a football match like the contribution of an outstanding and dynamic midfielder! Yet the quality of those performances is precisely the result of practice; the learning of the virtues which makes for excellence.

The same is true of our human living. At school we can learn early lessons in the acquisition and use of the virtues which we so much need in our society today. In our schools I trust that we are preparing the virtuoso performers for the future of our society.

Thank you for coming together this evening. Please pray for me as I take up these new responsibilities.

Now we turn in prayer to Mary, our sure Mother, who never turns away from us, but always leads us to her Son. Amen.

True dialogue and freedom
are in Christ

Mass of Installation, 21st May 2009

My brothers and sisters, I welcome you and I thank
you all for coming to Westminster Cathedral today. I
appreciate the presence and the prayers of each of
you. I greet and thank the Apostolic Nuncio, here
representing the Holy Father. Through him, I thank
Pope Benedict for the confidence that he has placed
in me in making this appointment and for his
blessing as I take it up.

I thank the Duke of Norfolk, the Earl Marshal, for
his presence and Lord Guthrie for representing the
Prince of Wales. We are honoured that you are here.
I am grateful also to the Rt Hon Paul Murphy, here
representing the Prime Minister. I appreciate too the
presence of politicians and civic leaders. I salute all
the bishops, priests and deacons who are here,
especially their Eminences Cardinal Mahoney from
Los Angeles, Cardinal O'Brien of St Andrews and
Edinburgh and Cardinal Seán Brady from Armagh. I
am so glad to see so many fellow church leaders and
leaders of other faiths, from the West Midlands and,
of course, from London. I thank Archbishop Rowan

for his gracious words of welcome, too. I thank the BBC for broadcasting this ceremony live on television and I greet all those joining us at home.

May I also express my deep appreciation to Cardinal Cormac Murphy-O'Connor for the very warm welcome that he has given to me and for his unfailing encouragement and support. Much more importantly, on behalf of so many, I want to salute the tremendous contribution he has made both to the Diocese of Westminster and to the Catholic Church nationally and internationally in his years as Archbishop of Westminster. His leadership has been unflinching and often very courageous, and I know that he will always have a special place in our affections and prayers. Your Eminence, we thank you!

Be open to God

The readings of the Scriptures that we have heard today centre on the figure of St Paul and we have heard Paul's own account of his dramatic conversion to Christ on the road to Damascus. It is a story of great power and one from which we can draw much encouragement.

In the first place, we learn that Paul was, "a zealous believer in God". His conversion then was not to belief in God but to belief in God's full presence in Jesus Christ.

This fact is important to us all. Through life-long belief, Paul was already open to the things of God, ready to recognise the touch of the divine in the unexpected.

This is the true nature of the belief in God: it opens us to all that lies beyond. It's a constant invitation to go beyond our immediate knowledge and awareness, and even our current commitments. Faith in God is not, as some would portray it today, a narrowing of the human mind or spirit. It is precisely the opposite. Faith in God is the gift that takes us beyond our limited self, with all its incessant demands. Faith opens us to a life that stretches us, enlightens us, and often springs surprises upon us. Such faith, like love, sees that which is invisible and lives by it.

God alone satisfies us

From Paul, then, we learn that the inner life of each one of us is crucial for our wellbeing. In our hearts we need the same openness to God as he had. This is expressed in daily moments of tranquillity and prayer when we regain a true sense of proportion, recognising afresh that God alone fulfils our deepest yearnings. Without such moments we quickly lose a sense of who we truly are.

It is before God that we gather here today, that he may touch and heal us.

But let us return to the Damascus road. Paul hears remarkable words: 'Saul, Saul, why are you persecuting me?' He recognises the voice of the Lord. Now he has to embrace the real identification between the risen Christ and the community of Christians he is persecuting. This is a troubling identification and it remains so today. Those who embrace belief in Christ Jesus are bound together in him, in a real yet incomplete way, in his body, the Church.

True social cohesion in Christ

So faith is never a solitary activity nor can it be simply private. Faith in Christ always draws us into a community and has a public dimension. This community of faith reaches beyond ethnicity, cultural difference and social division. It opens for us a vision of ourselves, and of our society, as having a single source and a single fulfilment. Indeed this vision of faith is expressed powerfully by St Paul when, in his letter to the Galatians, he says that in Christ 'There is no longer Jew or Greek, there is no longer slave or free, there is no longer male and female, for all of you are one in Christ Jesus' (*Ga* 3:28). This is a vision of true social cohesion, a promise which lies ahead and a signpost of which churches construct, Sunday by Sunday, with their communities of unity in diversity.

Faith builds community and it expresses itself in action. As a society, if we are to build on this gift of faith, we must respect its outward expression not only in honouring individual conscience but also in respecting the institutional integrity of the communities of faith in what they bring to public service and to the common good. Only in this way will individuals, families and faith communities become whole-hearted contributors to building the society we rightly seek.

True dialogue nurtured in faith and reason

Paul's conversion on the Damascus Road has a third aspect to it. His life is now centred on Christ and the Church. But he also grasps a truth about all creation. And he wants to share it.

In Christ, Paul's mind is now open, even to pagan philosophy. He now has the courage and the determination to go, for example, to the Areopagus in Athens and engage with the Greek philosophers. He struggles to find the language in which the insights and light of Christian faith can be brought into dialogue with the finest minds of his age.

As we know, his attempts at the Areopagus were not very successful. Yet the event is a reminder of the task facing us all: that of taking forward the intense dialogue across faiths and our contemporary world.

At the heart of Paul's effort in Athens was an appeal to reason. He did not seek to impose his beliefs, nor exploit anxiety or fear. Rather he had learned that his faith in Christ was compatible with the mind's capacity for reasoned thought. Indeed it complemented it. Some today propose that faith and reason are crudely opposed, with the fervour of faith replacing good reason. This is a reduction of both faith and reason. It inhibits not only our search for truth but also the possibility of real dialogue. In contrast, as Pope John Paul II memorably said: 'Faith and reason are the two wings on which the human spirit soars.' (*Fides et Ratio* n.1)

This dialogue needs to go beyond the superficial and the slogans. Respectful dialogue is crucial today and I salute all who seek to engage in it. In this the media have such an important part to play, not by accentuating difference and conflict, but by enhancing creative conversation. Let us be a society in which we genuinely listen to each other, in which sincere disagreement is not made out to be insult or harassment, in which reasoned principles are not construed as prejudice and in which we are prepared to attribute to each other the best and not the worst of motives. In these matters, we ourselves in the Churches have so much to learn and much to do. Yet we also have much to contribute.

Love reveals the truth of our humanity

Paul's experience of the Risen Christ fired him with a new enthusiasm, a powerful commitment to the truth of humanity made clear in Christ. It was this experience that enabled Paul to face all the challenges of life with what he called 'the supreme advantage of knowing Christ Jesus' (*Ph* 3:9).

This knowledge, which is of love, discloses the true worth of our humanity, our real dignity. This is its supreme advantage. For we human beings are not plasticine figures, to be moulded into shape at the hands of a political ideology, or under economic demands. Nor, at the end of the day, can we shape ourselves as we please, according to fashion or our untutored desires. We are not self-made. Our humanity, thankfully, is more deeply rooted and therefore more resilient. Indeed our humanity is a gift to be respected not only from its beginnings to its natural end, but also in the other ethical demands it places on us all. Tragically this humanity is often corrupted and distorted, by the misuse of power, by every evil and disaster. But so often we see that the miracle of love is stronger than such corruption. Love has the power to reveal again the depth and truth of our humanity. This is achieved in the enduring love of a parent for a wayward child, in the love of a friend or spouse faithful through every crisis, and in the unconditional love given by the saints, often to the poorest and most forgotten.

Christ, the manifesto of love

This is the love given supremely in Christ, and in him crucified. In him we find an unambiguous declaration, a manifesto, of our humanity in its full stature. And this manifesto is not a pamphlet but a person. It is, therefore, an invitation to know him and to be known by him, to love him and to be loved by him and so with him find the fullness of life.

In Christ we see a maturity of love that flowers in self-sacrifice and forgiveness; a maturity of power that never swerves from the ideal of service; a maturity of goodness that overcomes every temptation, and, of course, we see the ultimate victory of life over death itself. In Christ our true destiny is proclaimed in the resurrection of the dead and his promised eternal fulfilment of life in the new heaven and new earth.

True freedom and happiness are in Christ

The paradox of faith is that when we conform our lives to Christ then we gain our true freedom. Its fruit is profound and lasting happiness. This is the testimony of the true disciples of Jesus, great and humble alike. It is a testimony which shines across the ages and still in our day.

As I take up this new office, I ask for God's blessing. May we be deeply rooted in the Lord, and, at the same time, open to every prompting of the Holy Spirit. As St Paul tells us: 'Be united in your convictions and united in your love, with a common purpose and a common mind ... think of other people's interests first ... in your minds be the same as Christ Jesus' (*Ph* 2:2-5). May this be the experience of every family, in all of our schools, and in our parishes. From this wellspring emerges a profound desire to reach out to all, to engage in the work of building a world that reflects a little more closely the compassion, the justice, the tender mercy of God. This is the inspiration of Christian faith and one that serves our society well. This is the vision to which I readily commit myself today and for which I ask for your prayers and cooperation. Amen.

Christian marriage reveals the love of Christ

Pentecost Mass for married couples, 30th May 2009

Some time ago, on an economy flight from Rome, the air hostess was very chatty in her announcements. She even she told us that a married couple on board were celebrating their thirty-fifth wedding anniversary. They received sustained and heartfelt applause from all around the plane. Everyone appreciated their achievement. Sustaining a marriage for such a long time is not easy. It is evidence of a constant and mutual act of trust, combined with so many other virtues, too.

God accompanies the couple

The trust involved when a Christian couple undertake marriage is not only the trust they have in each other, but also the trust they have in God. They well understand, as people of faith, that in their marriage there is more than their own strength to draw on, more than their own capacity to love when they face difficulties. God is there with them and they minister God's grace to each other.

Now this is an important truth. God is at the heart of the promises which form a marriage. God is there to strengthen and sustain that marriage, to bless it and protect it. Without the acknowledgement of God's presence, a marriage is only half the reality it's supposed to be.

We all know how precious a marriage relationship can be. At times, that relationship can be the shining light of two lives, bringing fresh joy to every happiness and each small achievement. Yet we also know that, at other times, this relationship can become lost in a fog of mutual indifference. Sometimes that relationship becomes a treacherous quicksand, to be negotiated only with extreme care. Sometimes, as we know too well, that relationship, and the marriage itself, tragically lies in ruins.

But in all of this, God is still present. In many marriages God's presence is entirely out of sight, because it was never understood or invoked. Indeed, the understanding that God is involved in a marriage, giving it a different kind of permanence, a different kind of depth, is so foreign to our world that even we people of faith might be in danger of forgetting it, too. Yet a marriage without God is no more than a matter of personal choice and personal satisfaction. In those circumstances, there is far less reason to work hard at a marriage when that initial satisfaction has gone and the personal choice seems to have been a mistake.

So today, in this wonderful celebration, we again affirm that only the presence of God makes clear the true nature of marriage. Only God's grace can complete and renew such a relationship. Only then does a relationship become a sacrament which can speak eloquently to our world of the full vocation of married life.

The Church's vision of marriage

This vision of marriage lies at the centre of the Church's teaching. Indeed, without the firm understanding and belief that God is at the heart of every marriage, much of that teaching seems unreasonable and out-dated. The permanence of marriage, which guides the Church's teaching towards those in second marriages, is rooted in the sacramental presence of God in a valid marriage. The call of the Church to a man and a woman to marry rather than simply live together in a private arrangement is based on the same conviction that God's acknowledged presence is essential for a truly mature human relationship of husband and wife. To fail to see this truth inevitably leads us to see marriage as a human value only and, in the last resort, disposable and replaceable.

Today I congratulate you all on the years of faithfulness which lie behind your presence here. I'm told that you represent a total of over 45,000 years of faithful married life. You must have some stories to tell! Some present here today are celebrating over 60 years of marriage. Indeed two couples are celebrating 70 years of married life! Congratulations to you all.

In faith, we strive to fulfil the Church's teaching, doing our best to bring our lives into line with God's will, in all the ways open to us. We know that this is our best chance of fulfilment. In every life, this is a long and slow process. In marriage it certainly can be very testing. So today, in this Mass, and in many other ways, it is important that we promote marriage, offering real encouragement to young people and young couples to make the journey to marriage. We must show acceptance and support to those who have experienced failure in their marriage. We are to encourage them in their life of faith, in all the ways the Church shows to us. We never give up, never abandon hope or effort, knowing always that the Lord is with us, drawing us in His own mysterious ways closer to Himself and to those who truly sustain and guard us.

The Holy Family – an image of every family

On the cover of the Mass booklet – so beautifully prepared – is the photograph of the wonderful image of the Holy Family. Joseph and Mary present to us their Son. Throughout His childhood they nurtured Him and protected Him from danger. In doing so they were serving the whole human family, for they were nurturing and presenting the true hope of the world, the eternal Word of God in our flesh.

In this, the Holy Family is an image of every family. As you travel through life, so often difficult and distressing, you too carry with you the same eternal Word, the same Lord of life. Every family, with a marriage at its heart, makes its journey with Jesus present in its midst. In family life, then, we carry Him with us. We show Him to each other. Day by day we spell out, as best we can, the truth that God considers every moment of this life worthwhile, that God is committed to our well-being and joy, that God will never desert us or turn away. This is the reality of faith we try to make present for each other. In this way we proclaim and pass on our faith.

The family as a domestic Church

In this sense, the family is indeed the domestic church, proclaiming the living presence of our Saviour in every moment, striving to live by his love and praising him readily in daily prayer. Constantly He proves to be your Saviour, your Light and your Hope.

To embrace this reality of God's presence within marriage and family life is not just for each day. To embrace this presence is to be open to the promise of eternity. Marriage and family life are not just for now. Husbands and wives are committed to each other, and to their children, in order to get each other to heaven. Daily life is the ladder of our ascent.

Please look again at the mosaic of the Holy Family. See the central position given to the dove, hovering above that family, inspiring its joy and goodness.

Holy Spirit – source of peace and happiness

This is the Holy Spirit, whose coming we celebrate so readily at this Feast of Pentecost. This Spirit is the author of the goodness we seek for each other, the fountain of all those gifts which we so need for our daily peace and happiness. The fruits of the Spirit are known to us:

Charity: that conscious choice to love one's spouse for the person they actually are.

Joy: the pleasure we take in each other's abiding goodness.

Peace: the fruit of a determination to see things together, to do things together.

Patience: not just putting up with things but consciously being one with Christ in bearing the cross of suffering and disappointment.

Kindness: that sympathetic concern for all who are in need.

Goodness: trying to become a gift for each other, and not a demand!

Faithfulness: going beyond the demands of justice and rights and being ready to forgive, again and again!

Gentleness: getting beyond the satisfaction of provoking a response and allowing the space and time that is needed.

Self-control: avoiding excess, embracing simplicity of life, caring for each other physically with deference and great joy.

As St Paul writes: 'There is no law against such things!' (*Ga* 5:23). On the contrary, they are the recipe for holiness, a holiness of the home, the holiness of our shared journey to heaven.

These are the fruits of the gift of the Holy Spirit for which we pray with a special eagerness today. We know our need, for we too are very much part of the 'entire creation', which is groaning as we wait to be set free. We too cannot find the right words with which to pray and gladly rely on the Holy Spirit to express our longing for the Lord 'in a way that could never be put into words' (*Rm* 8:26).

Indeed, Lord, we are thirsty for you! We come to drink of your living water that our lives may be pleasing to you and a witness to your love for all, without exception, in our world. Amen.

Let us create places of welcome

Mass of Welcome, May and June 2009

It is a great joy for me to celebrate this Mass of welcome with you. Thank you for your warm welcome. Thank you for coming here this evening. This is a moment in which we celebrate our faith and seek to renew that faith in the Risen Lord and the life to which he invites us.

We celebrate this Mass in this Easter period, rich in meaning and hope. We have just celebrated the Feast of the Ascension, in which our final destiny is revealed. We are also celebrating the great Feast of Pentecost, in which we receive all the means we need in order to achieve that destiny.

Christ's Ascension: God alone is our fulfilment

Often, when on a journey as a child – as many children do – I would constantly ask: 'Are we there yet?' When walking in the hills, it is easy to get disheartened by the number of false summits that have to be climbed! The same is true in life as a whole. We can often end up wondering about the point of it all.

In the Ascension of the Lord, however, the final point and purpose of our daily pilgrimage is made clear. The words of the liturgy tell us unambiguously: 'Where he the head has gone, we the body will certainly follow' (*Preface*).

Our fulfilment lies in finally coming into the presence of God. He alone is our fulfilment, our complete satisfaction, the answer to every profound and unsettling need which we feel. In his presence we shall be both fully known and fully loved. What is more we shall both fully know God and be fully taken up into the love of God whom we shall see!

These are wonders which we only occasionally glimpse. A glimpse is all we achieve here in this world. But the glimpses are there.

Occasionally, despite all our troubles and anxieties, we have a profound sense of being at peace. This might come for us in precious moments of prayer. At times, we will experience a deep sense of community, of being together in a wide and embracing family, or of being profoundly united with the one we love. And just occasionally we have a sense of the wholeness and goodness of life, perhaps in moments in which we glimpse the beauty which is so gracefully traced in our world.

These are no more than fleeting glimpses of the destiny that lies ahead, revealed for us in the ascent of the Lord to the glory of heaven. This is the hope which we renew within ourselves today.

Pentecost: God's gift of love

Also, in this time of the Church's year, we are given an understanding, and the very gift, of the means we need in order to make our journey on earth. This gift is, of course, the very love that our Lord constantly offers to us. It is the gift of the Holy Spirit, the Lord's love in action in our world and in our lives. In just a few moments we shall sing of our longing to receive that gift: 'Come down O Love Divine, visit thou this soul of mine!'

These means are, of course, opened for us in the life of the Church. We receive these gifts and seek their growth within us in our shared life, by working together in the activities of faith, in our striving for understanding and truth, in our attempts to form right judgements and, most of all, in our service of others. In all these ways we draw life from our Lord, the life of the Spirit, so that we can be one with Him in all things.

Our mission to serve

This is the mission we receive. This is the mission in which we rejoice. St Peter speaks of this mission in powerful words:

'You are a chosen race': we have received the gift of faith; this is our great privilege. 'You are a royal priesthood': it is our privilege to bring all things to

God, through our prayer, through our daily offering. 'You are a consecrated nation': God has blessed us so as to be His instruments in our world in a particular way. Each of us has a calling and a task. 'You are a people set apart to sing the praises of God.' This is what we do this evening, and with great joy! (cf. 1 *Pt* 2:9).

In the Gospel passage we have heard, St Matthew speaks of disciples receiving their mission, one that is shared with us too: 'All authority on heaven and earth is given to you', 'Go out to all nations', 'Baptise them,' and, 'Teach them all I have commanded you.' (cf. *Mt* 28:17)

This commissioning of the disciples is preceded by a little scene which is always of real comfort to me. The disciples come out to meet the risen Lord. They kneel before him. But then we read: 'Although some hesitated.' How consoling! Such hesitation and doubt is so much a part of our journey of faith!

Remember that at the beginning of the Gospel, St Matthew tells us that the wise men came and knelt before Jesus. Now, at the end of his Gospel, the message is the same: those who are wise come and kneel before the Lord – although many of us will hesitate!

Crossing the threshold

In recent days I have been reflecting on the Mass of Installation in Westminster Cathedral. It was a wonderful experience! It was an experience of truly being together. Here was the whole Church. Pope Benedict was represented; there were bishops from around the world; people, priests, deacons, religious were all present. This was a great gathering pointing to the profound unity which is ours in God. And, in a special way, I sensed the presence of Cardinal Hume, too.

The Mass was also an experience of real joy in the Lord and of exuberance in his presence. During that Liturgy, we offered God our best: the best music, vestments, and liturgy – everything! And that is always the fitting way for us to celebrate the Mass.

For me, the most powerful and unforgettable moment was when I paused and stayed kneeling in the doorway of the Cathedral. At that moment I had a profound sense of being in a holy place.

Indeed, the threshold of the church is always holy. It is often a place of diffidence, of lack of assuredness. It is a place in which some hesitate. It is as far as some ever get. Yet it is a holy place, where God's Spirit is at work. It is in fact a point at which the world, in all its diversity, meets and mingles with the visible things of God.

Parishes are a place of welcome

The threshold of the church is the place where we are open to receive many of the good things which the Holy Spirit works in the world. It is the place where we are always to show a readiness to welcome all who come.

Recently Pope Benedict spoke of the openness needed in parish life: 'The parish should not be a circle closed in on itself. We (our parishes) have our customs. But still we must be open and endeavour to create vestibules, that is, places of welcome which will draw others closer.'

Pope Benedict talked about the need for every parish to reach out beyond its regular church-goers to create spaces and places in which others can come together to experience the life of faith, prayer and the word of God. He added: 'Someone who comes from afar cannot immediately enter parish life, which already has its own customs.'

These were some of the thoughts in my mind and heart as I knelt in that doorway, at the threshold, and asked God's blessing on my own goings and comings.

Let our hearts be open to others

Our hearts do need to be open: with an openness to receive and a warm welcome to offer. Indeed there are many times and places in our lives when we stand on the threshold, when we are talking with people for whom the life of the Church is distant, or who have distanced themselves from it. These are the moments which we must hold to be holy, in which the Holy Spirit is at work, but which we must not hurry, or seek to conclude. The threshold of the heart, too, is a holy place.

I hope that in the life of every parish we can be sensitive and attentive at all times, not turning people away or unwittingly shutting any door on them.

Yet, let us also remember that once we cross this threshold of the Church and enter into its life, new expectations are accepted and new demands are made of us. And when we cross this holy threshold, then we also find fresh help, strength and consolation. This is the true mystery of faith, to which we can welcome many.

I thank you for your welcome. I look forward to our life together in the years to come. May the Lord bless us all as we strive to serve Him in all we do. Amen.